LARRY ELLISON

The Oracle Behind

Tech Dominance

Veron Allen

Table of Content

Introduction

In the vast and ever-evolving chronicles of technology, few individuals have left an imprint as profound and enduring as Larry Ellison. As the co-founder and former CEO of Oracle Corporation, one of the world's largest software companies, Ellison stands as a towering figure in the annals of innovation and entrepreneurialism. His journey from humble beginnings to the pinnacle of the tech industry is a captivating tale of unwavering determination, audacious risk-taking, and a visionary's unwavering belief in the transformative power of technology.

Ellison's impact on the world of technology is immeasurable. He is widely recognized as the pioneer of relational databases, a groundbreaking concept that revolutionized the way businesses manage and analyze data. His leadership at Oracle has transformed the company into a global powerhouse, shaping the very fabric of the digital age. Oracle's software products, ranging from enterprise resource planning (ERP) systems to customer relationship management (CRM) solutions, have become indispensable tools for countless organizations worldwide.

Beyond his business acumen, Ellison is also known for his philanthropy, his love of sailing, and his passion for pushing the boundaries of human ingenuity. He has generously supported educational initiatives, medical research, and environmental conservation efforts through his charitable foundation. As an avid sailor, he has competed in some of the world's most prestigious yacht races, including the America's Cup. And as a futurist, he has invested in cutting-edge technologies such as artificial intelligence and renewable energy, demonstrating his unwavering commitment to shaping the future.

In this comprehensive biography, we will delve into the life and legacy of Larry Ellison, exploring his triumphs, setbacks, and the profound impact he has made on the world. From his early days as a programmer to his ascent as a tech titan, this is the story of a man who dared to dream big and changed the course of technological history. Through interviews with Ellison himself, his colleagues, and industry experts, we will gain a deeper understanding of his motivations, his leadership style, and his vision for the future.

1

The Early Years

Larry Ellison's birth took place on the 17th of August in the year 1944, within the Bronx borough of New York City. His mother, Florence Spellman, was an unwed teenager who gave him up for adoption nine months later. Ellison was adopted by his aunt and uncle, Lillian and Louis Ellison, who lived in Chicago. His adoptive father was a Russian Jewish immigrant who worked as a real estate agent, while his adoptive mother was a homemaker.

Ellison's early years were marked by both challenges and opportunities. He was a bright and curious child, but he struggled academically, particularly in math. He also had a difficult relationship with his adoptive father, who was often and critical. Despite these challenges, Ellison developed a strong work ethic and a passion for learning.

At the age of 12, Ellison's family moved to California. He attended the University of Illinois at Urbana-Champaign for two years, but dropped out in 1964 to pursue a career in computer programming. He moved to Berkeley, California, and worked as a programmer for several companies, including Ampex and Wells Fargo.

In the year 1977, Ellison, alongside Bob Miner and Ed Oates, established the company known as Oracle Corporation.The company's first product was a relational database management system called Oracle Database. Ellison's vision for Oracle was to create a database that could handle large amounts of data and be used by multiple users simultaneously. This was a revolutionary concept at the time, and it quickly made Oracle one of the leading players in the database market.

Ellison's early years were geprägt by both struggle and success. He overcame personal challenges and academic difficulties to pursue his passion for computer programming. His determination and vision laid the foundation for what would become one of the most successful technology companies in the world.

Ellison's childhood and education

Larry Ellison's childhood was marked by both challenges and opportunities. He was born to an unwed teenage mother and given up for adoption. He was adopted by his aunt and uncle, who lived in Chicago. His adoptive father was a Russian Jewish immigrant who worked as a real estate agent, while his adoptive mother was a homemaker.

Ellison's early years were difficult. He struggled academically, particularly in math, and he had a difficult relationship with his adoptive father. Despite these challenges, Ellison developed a strong work ethic and a passion for learning. He was also a gifted athlete, and he excelled in baseball and basketball.

At the age of 12, Ellison's family moved to California. He attended the University of Illinois at Urbana-Champaign for two years, but dropped out in 1964 to pursue a career in computer programming. He moved to Berkeley, California, and worked as a programmer for several companies, including Ampex and Wells Fargo.

Ellison's formal education may have been cut short, but he continued to learn and develop his skills throughout his career. He is known for his voracious appetite for knowledge and his ability to quickly grasp complex technical concepts. Ellison is also a self-taught sailor, and he has competed in some of the world's most prestigious yacht races, including the America's Cup.

Ellison's childhood and education experiences shaped him into the man he is today. He is a determined and resilient individual with a strong work ethic and a passion for learning. He is also a visionary leader with a knack for seeing the potential in new technologies.

Interest in technology and hacking

Larry Ellison's interest in technology began at a young age. He was fascinated by how computers worked, and he loved to take them apart and put them back together. He also enjoyed playing video games and writing his own software programs.

In the early 1970s, Ellison became involved in the hacking community. He was drawn to the challenge of breaking into computer systems and exploring their vulnerabilities. He also enjoyed the camaraderie of other hackers, and he quickly became a respected member of the community.

Ellison's hacking skills proved to be valuable when he co-founded Oracle Corporation in 1977. He used his knowledge of computer systems to develop Oracle Database, a relational database management system that was far more powerful and efficient than anything else on the market at the time.

Ellison's interest in technology and hacking has continued throughout his career. He is known for his love of gadgets and his willingness to experiment with new technologies. He is also a strong supporter of open source software and the hacker culture.

Ellison's interest in technology and hacking has been a major driving force behind his success. He has used his knowledge and skills to create one of the most successful technology companies in the world. He is also a generous supporter of the hacker community and the open source movement.

Moving to California

In 1958, when Ellison was 12 years old, his family moved from Chicago to California. They settled in the San Francisco Bay Area, which was then emerging as a hub for the computer industry.

Ellison's move to California had a profound impact on his life. He was exposed to the latest computer technologies and the vibrant hacker culture of the Bay Area. He also met some of the people who would later become his partners in founding Oracle Corporation.

Ellison attended the University of Illinois at Urbana-Champaign for two years, but dropped out in 1964 to pursue a career in computer programming. He moved back to California and worked as a programmer for several companies, including Ampex and Wells Fargo.

In 1977, Ellison co-founded Oracle Corporation in California. The company quickly became one of the leading players in the database market, and Ellison became one of the richest and most influential people in the tech industry.

Ellison's move to California was a pivotal moment in his life. It brought him to the center of the computer revolution and gave him the opportunity to meet the people and develop the skills that would lead to his success.

Here are some of the factors that influenced Ellison's decision to move to California:

· The Bay Area was a hub for the computer industry, and Ellison was eager to be part of the action.

• Ellison was drawn to the hacker culture of the Bay Area, and he wanted to learn from and collaborate with other hackers.

• Ellison was looking for a place where he could start his own business, and he believed that California was the best place to do that.

Ellison's move to California was a risky one, but it paid off in a big way. He became one of the most successful entrepreneurs in the world, and he helped to make California the global center of the tech industry.

2

The Oracle Years

Larry Ellison, the co-founder of Oracle Corporation, has had a remarkable career that spans several decades. He served as the CEO of Oracle from **1977 to 2014** and is currently the chief technology officer and executive chairman. Known for his business acumen, Ellison led Oracle through a series of strategic acquisitions, including notable companies like PeopleSoft, Siebel, BEA, and Sun Microsystems. His early work at Ampex Corporation, where he worked on a database project for the CIA named "Oracle," set the stage for his future success.

Ellison's personal life is just as colorful as his professional one. Born on August 17, 1944, in New York City, he was adopted by his aunt and uncle after contracting pneumonia at nine months old. He grew up in Chicago's South Shore and later pursued higher education, though he did not complete a degree. Ellison is also known for his philanthropy, his passion for yachting and aviation, and for owning 98% of Lānaʻi, the sixth-largest island in the Hawaiian Islands.

As of March 2024, Larry Ellison is one of the wealthiest individuals in the world, with an estimated net worth of $130 billion according to the Bloomberg Billionaires Index, and $154 billion according to Forbes. His influence extends beyond Oracle, as he continues to shape the tech industry with his innovative spirit and strategic vision.

Co-founding Oracle Corporation

Co-founding Oracle Corporation is a significant milestone in the history of technology. Larry Ellison, along with Bob Miner and Ed Oates, founded the company in 1977 under the name Software Development Laboratories (SDL). The trio's vision was to create a relational database management system (RDBMS), which was inspired by Edgar F. Codd's research on the relational model for databases.

Their first project was a database for the CIA, which they named "Oracle." The success of this project led to the development of the Oracle Database, which became the company's flagship product. In 1982, SDL changed its name to Oracle Systems Corporation to align itself more closely with its primary product.

Oracle Corporation grew rapidly during the 1980s, becoming a publicly traded company and expanding its product line to include not just databases but also tools and applications. The company's growth was fueled by Ellison's aggressive marketing strategies and his foresight in recognizing the potential of network computing.

Ellison's leadership and Oracle's innovative products have had a profound impact on the IT industry, making Oracle one of the largest software companies in the world. The company's commitment to innovation continues to this day, with investments in cloud computing and other emerging technologies. Ellison's role in co-founding Oracle Corporation and his continued involvement in its evolution remain central to the company's success story.

Developing Oracle's database software

Developing Oracle's database software is a comprehensive process that involves a deep understanding of database concepts, SQL, PL/SQL programming, and the Oracle Database environment. Oracle provides a rich set of tools and features to support the development and management of robust, secure, scalable, and high-performance database applications. Here's a detailed guide on how you can develop with Oracle's database software:

Understanding Oracle Database

Before diving into development, it's crucial to understand the architecture and core components of Oracle Database. Oracle Database is a multi-model database management system that supports SQL, JSON, XML, and more. It's designed for enterprise grid computing, which provides the most flexible and cost-effective way to manage information and applications.

Setting Up the Development Environment

1.**Install Oracle Database:** You can download and install Oracle Database from Oracle's official website. Choose the version that suits your requirements, such as 11gR2, 19c, 21c, or the latest 23c.

2.**Download SQL Developer:** Oracle SQL Developer is a free, integrated development environment that simplifies the development and management of Oracle Database. It offers a worksheet for running queries and scripts, a DBA console for managing the database, a reports interface, a complete data modeling solution, and a migration platform for moving your 3rd party databases to Oracle.

3.**Explore Oracle SQLcl:** For command-line enthusiasts, Oracle SQL Developer Command Line (SQLcl) is a modern command-line interface for Oracle Database. It's lightweight and supports automatic formatting for various output formats like CSV, XML, JSON, and more.

Learning SQL and PL/SQL

SQL and PL/SQL are the primary languages used for interacting with Oracle Database:

-**SQL**: Structured Query Language (SQL) is used for querying, updating, and managing data in Oracle Database. You'll need to become proficient in writing SQL statements to perform CRUD (Create, Read, Update, Delete) operations.

-**PL/SQL**:Procedural Language/SQL (PL/SQL) is Oracle's procedural extension to SQL. It's used to write complex stored procedures, functions, packages, and triggers. Learning PL/SQL will enable you to create sophisticated business logic within the database.

Database Application Development

With the knowledge of SQL and PL/SQL, you can begin developing database applications:

-**Data Modeling:** Use Oracle SQL Developer Data Modeler to design and implement your database schema. It allows you to create logical, relational, physical, multi-dimensional, and data type models.

-**Application Development**: Develop your application using Oracle's tools and frameworks. You can build SaaS apps, microservices, and mobile applications using technologies like Kubernetes, Docker, and Oracle Autonomous Database.

-**Performance Tuning**: Optimize the performance of your database applications by analyzing execution plans, optimizing SQL statements, and properly indexing your database.

-**Security**: Implement security measures such as encryption, access controls, and auditing to protect your data and comply with regulations.

-**Testing and Deployment**: Thoroughly test your applications and deploy them to your target environment, whether it's on-premises or in the Oracle Cloud.

Resources and Documentation

Oracle provides extensive documentation and resources to help developers:

-**Oracle Documentation**: Refer to Oracle's official documentation for detailed information on developing Oracle Database applications.

-**Oracle Community**: Join the Oracle Developer Community to connect with other developers, ask questions, and share knowledge.

-**Sample Code**: Access sample code and examples on Oracle's website and GitHub to learn from real-world applications.

Developing with Oracle's database software is a journey of continuous learning and improvement. By leveraging Oracle's powerful tools and resources, you can create high-quality database applications that meet the demands of modern businesses. Remember to stay updated with the latest Oracle releases and features to ensure your skills and applications remain relevant and efficient.

Rise as a major player

Larry Ellison's rise as a major player in the tech industry is a story of ambition, innovation, and strategic growth. As the co-founder of Oracle Corporation, Ellison transformed the company from a startup with just three programmers into the largest database software supplier and the second-largest supplier of business applications. His journey began in 1977, and through a series of strategic acquisitions, including companies like PeopleSoft, Siebel Systems, and Sun

Microsystems, Oracle reached a market cap of roughly $185 billion with some 130,000 employees by 2014.

Ellison's approach to business has been characterized by aggressive competition and a focus on growth through acquisitions. His leadership style and vision for Oracle have played a significant role in shaping the company's direction and success. Under his guidance, Oracle has become a powerhouse in the software industry, known for its comprehensive and integrated suite of applications and platforms.

Outside of Oracle, Ellison has also made significant investments in various sectors, including a major investment in Tesla and reportedly having a seat on Apple's board of directors for a while. His interests extend beyond the tech world, with indulgences in yacht racing and owning nearly an entire Hawaiian island.

Ellison's son, David Ellison, has also made a name for himself in the entertainment industry. David's production company, Skydance Media, has become a powerful and profitable maker of big-budget movies and TV shows, with hits like "Top Gun: Maverick" and "The Family Plan" under its belt. David Ellison's success in Hollywood and potential bid for Paramount Global could further elevate the Ellison family's status as major players in both technology and entertainment.

Larry Ellison's rise is a testament to his relentless pursuit of excellence and strategic thinking, making him one of the most influential figures in the world of technology and business.

3

The Rise of the Cloud

Larry Ellison's involvement with cloud computing is a fascinating narrative of skepticism turned into strategic embrace. Initially, Ellison was known for his critical views on cloud computing, famously dismissing it as "complete gibberish" and "insane". However, as the industry evolved, so did Ellison's stance. He went from questioning the cloud's viability to claiming it was his idea, citing his early investment in NetSuite as an example of pioneering software-as-a-service (SaaS). Ellison's Oracle Corporation, where he serves as the Chief Technology Officer and Executive Chairman, has since become a significant player in the cloud services market. Oracle's cloud services encompass a wide range of applications, from enterprise resource planning (ERP) to human capital management (HCM), and customer relationship management (CRM). Ellison's vision for the cloud has been one of a second-generation cloud that is purpose-built for the enterprise, offering advanced technology and enhanced security compared to its competitors.

Discussing the future of cloud computing, Ellison referred to the concept of an "internet of clouds," which would create great value for customers by moving away from the original "walled gardens" that promoted isolation and complexity. This idea aligns with the current trend towards multi-cloud strategies, where businesses leverage the strengths of different cloud providers to optimize their operations.

Ellison's shift from a cloud critic to a cloud visionary underscores the dynamic nature of the tech industry and the importance of adapting to new paradigms. His journey with cloud computing reflects Oracle's broader strategy of innovation and adaptation, ensuring the company remains at the forefront of technological advancements. Ellison's ability to recognize the potential of cloud technology and pivot Oracle's focus towards it has been a key factor in the company's continued success and influence in the tech sector.

Oracle's entry into cloud computing

Oracle's entry into cloud computing, spearheaded by Larry Ellison, marked a significant shift in the company's strategy. Initially, Oracle was known for its database software and on-premises solutions. However, the landscape of technology was rapidly changing with the advent of cloud computing, and Oracle had to adapt to maintain its market position.

In 2010, Oracle made a pivotal move by acquiring Sun Microsystems, which gave them control over key technologies like Java and MySQL. This acquisition was a stepping stone for Oracle's future in cloud services. By 2016, Oracle announced its fully integrated cloud offering, combining Software as a Service (SaaS), Platform as a

Service (PaaS), and Infrastructure as a Service (IaaS), thus establishing its presence in the cloud computing market.

Larry Ellison's vision for Oracle's cloud computing was to create a second-generation cloud that was purpose-built for the enterprise. This new cloud was designed to be more technologically advanced and secure than the existing solutions in the market. Ellison emphasized features like impenetrable barriers, autonomous robots, dedicated cloud control computers, and a high-speed RDMA network to differentiate Oracle's cloud services.

Moreover, Oracle's cloud strategy included forming partnerships to enhance its offerings. For example, a partnership with Microsoft allowed Oracle's customers to access Oracle database programs running on Oracle's cloud infrastructure but deployed in Microsoft's Azure data centers. This strategic move showcased Oracle's commitment to providing flexible and innovative cloud solutions to meet the diverse needs of its customers.

Ellison's leadership and strategic decisions were crucial in transitioning Oracle into a cloud computing powerhouse. Despite initial skepticism, Oracle's cloud services have shown rapid growth, especially with the demand for AI cloud offerings, which have been unusually strong for an unseasoned cloud provider[1]. Today, Oracle's cloud infrastructure, known as Oracle Cloud Infrastructure (OCI), offers a comprehensive range of services, including compute, storage, and networking, tailored to meet the needs of enterprise-level customers.

Larry Ellison's impact on cloud computing is evident through Oracle's development and continuous innovation in the cloud sector, ensuring that the company remains a major player in the ever-evolving tech industry. Oracle's journey into cloud computing reflects Ellison's ability to adapt and lead the company through significant technological transformations.

Ellison's vision for the future

Larry Ellison's vision for the future is a testament to his forward-thinking and innovative mindset, particularly in the realm of cloud computing and artificial intelligence. At Oracle CloudWorld 2023, Ellison shared his insights on the impact and potential of generative AI, which can generate language, images, music, code, and even drugs. He emphasized how Oracle is leveraging generative AI to transform its cloud infrastructure, database, application development, and data intelligence platforms.

Ellison highlighted several key aspects of Oracle's future direction:

-**Generative AI Integration**: Oracle is embedding generative AI into its cloud services to help customers solve complex problems. This includes tools for improving healthcare, automating application development, and even aiding in food production.

-**Cloud Infrastructure Advancements**: Oracle's second-generation cloud infrastructure is designed to be faster and more cost-effective than other clouds, thanks to ultrafast remote data memory access (RDMA) networking and connections to NVIDIA GPUs in superclusters. This infrastructure is poised to efficiently train generative AI models at twice the speed and less than half the cost of other clouds.

-**Application Development Transformation** : The use of generative AI is changing how Oracle develops new products. For instance, Oracle APEX's application generator allows for faster development with smaller teams, and the code generated by generative AI tools based on developer prompts helps reduce security flaws.

-**Healthcare Innovation**: Ellison has also expressed Oracle's commitment to advancing global healthcare. He envisions a more effective, efficient, and secure healthcare system that improves health outcomes globally, leveraging Oracle's technology to achieve this goal.

Ellison's vision for the future is not just limited to technological advancements but also includes a broader impact on society. He sees Oracle's innovations as a means to address some of the most pressing challenges faced by industries and communities worldwide. As Oracle continues to push the boundaries of what's possible with cloud and AI, Ellison's vision is set to shape the future of technology and its application across various domains.

Impact on the industry

Larry Ellison's impact on the tech industry is profound and multifaceted. As the co-founder of Oracle Corporation, he has been a driving force behind some of the most significant technological advancements in the past few decades. Here are some key aspects of Ellison's influence:

Revolutionizing Database Management

Ellison's creation of the Oracle database management system revolutionized the way companies handle data. By making data management faster and more efficient, Oracle paved the way for a technological revolution, inspiring other companies to develop similar systems and contributing to the overall growth of the industry.

Strategic Acquisitions and Growth

Ellison's strategic acquisitions have been pivotal in Oracle's success. By acquiring companies like Sun Microsystems, Hyperion Solutions, Retek, Siebel Systems, and PeopleSoft, Oracle expanded its market reach and diversified its product offerings. These moves allowed Oracle to enter new markets and offer a comprehensive range of solutions, solidifying its position as a tech giant.

Fostering Innovation in Silicon Valley

Oracle's success under Ellison's leadership contributed to the growth of Silicon Valley, turning it into a hub for innovation and entrepreneurship. Ellison's involvement in various initiatives, including the America's Cup sailing competition, helped to raise the profile of Silicon Valley as a center for technological advancement.

Early Recognition of the Internet's Potential

Ellison was one of the early tech leaders to recognize the potential of the internet. His development of database management systems set industry precedents and inspired other companies to explore the possibilities of internet-based technologies.

Advancing Cloud Computing

Ellison's foresight positioned Oracle to handle the growing demand for cloud-based enterprise technology. Notably, during the COVID-19 pandemic, Zoom Video Communications chose Oracle Cloud Infrastructure to support their services, validating Ellison's strategic decisions and Oracle's capabilities in the cloud sector.

Visionary Leadership

Ellison's visionary leadership transformed Oracle from a startup into a global tech powerhouse. His ability to outmaneuver rivals and his early recognition of emerging technologies played a crucial role in shaping the tech industry and Oracle's trajectory.

Larry Ellison's legacy in the tech industry is characterized by his relentless pursuit of innovation, strategic business acumen, and the ability to foresee and adapt to technological shifts. His contributions have not only shaped Oracle's history but have also had a lasting impact on the broader technology landscape.

4

The America's Cup

Larry Ellison, co-founder and former CEO of Oracle Corporation, has a long and storied history with the America's Cup, the world's most prestigious sailing race. Ellison first became involved with the America's Cup in 1995, when he founded Oracle Team USA. Since then, Oracle Team USA has won the America's Cup twice, in 2010 and 2013.

Ellison is a passionate sailor and a fierce competitor. He has invested heavily in Oracle Team USA, providing the team with the resources and support it needs to be successful. Ellison is also known for his aggressive tactics on the race course. In 2013, Oracle Team USA came from behind to defeat Team New Zealand in a dramatic come-from-behind victory.

Ellison's involvement with the America's Cup has helped to raise the profile of the race and attract new fans. He has also been a vocal advocate for changes to the America's Cup format, including the introduction of foiling catamarans in 2013.

In 2021, Ellison announced that he was stepping down as CEO of Oracle Team USA. However, he remains committed to the team and to the America's Cup. He is currently serving as the team's chairman and is actively involved in planning for the 37th America's Cup, which will be held in Barcelona, Spain in 2024.

Ellison's Impact on the America's Cup

Ellison has had a significant impact on the America's Cup. He has helped to raise the profile of the race, attract new fans, and introduce new technologies. Ellison is also known for his aggressive tactics on the race course, which have made him one of the most successful skippers in the history of the America's Cup.

Here are some of Ellison's most notable contributions to the America's Cup:

• Founded Oracle Team USA in 1995

• Led Oracle Team USA to victory in the America's Cup in 2010 and 2013

• Advocated for changes to the America's Cup format, including the introduction of foiling catamarans

• Invested heavily in Oracle Team USA, providing the team with the resources and support it needs to be successful

Larry Ellison is a passionate sailor and a fierce competitor. His involvement with the America's Cup has helped to raise the profile of the race and attract new fans. Ellison is also known for his aggressive tactics on the race course, which have made him one of the most successful skippers in the history of the America's Cup.

Ellison's involvement in yacht racing

Larry Ellison's involvement in yacht racing is marked by his passion for sailing and his contributions to the sport's technological advancements. Ellison's journey in yacht racing began with his success on his 78-foot yacht, Sayonara, where he won five Maxi World Championships. His passion for sailing led him to the America's Cup, where he won twice with Oracle Team USA in 2010 and 2013.

Ellison's impact on sailing extends beyond his victories. He has been instrumental in developing sailing at the highest levels by creating pathways for younger sailors. This includes the inclusion of the Red Bull Youth America's Cup in San Francisco and the development of SailGP, an international racing series started in 2019 alongside Russel Coutts. SailGP uses F50 foiling catamarans, the fastest class of boat in history, with regattas held across the globe. Ellison pledged financial support for a duration of five years to aid the series in reaching a point where it could sustain itself.

Moreover, Ellison's Oracle team introduced kite yachting into the America's Cup environment in 2002, achieving kite sail flying lasting about 30 minutes during testing in New Zealand[1]. His vision and investment have had a profound impact on the sport of sailing in the United States, pushing the boundaries of what's possible and contributing to the sport's evolution.

Ellison's daring and defiance have also marked his journey to the pinnacle of sailing. His approach to the America's Cup has transformed the regatta from a highbrow sport to a death-defying drag race, remaking its very nature and increasing its appeal and excitement.

Larry Ellison's involvement in yacht racing has not only brought him personal victories but has also significantly influenced the sport, leading to technological innovations and new opportunities for upcoming sailors. His legacy in yacht racing is one of passion, innovation, and a relentless pursuit of excellence.

Success and controversies

Larry Ellison, the co-founder of Oracle Corporation, is a figure synonymous with success and controversy in the tech industry. His journey from the creation of Oracle to becoming one of the wealthiest individuals in the world is marked by a series of bold decisions, aggressive business tactics, and a flair for innovation.

Successes:

-**Oracle's Growth**: Ellison's leadership has been instrumental in Oracle's rise as a leading technology firm. His autocratic decision-making style steered the company through various industry challenges, ensuring its position as a leading technology firm.

-**Visionary Leadership**: Ellison's early recognition of the internet's potential and his strategic acquisitions have solidified

Oracle's market position and expanded its product offerings.

-**Technological Innovation:** Ellison's foresight positioned Oracle to handle the growing demand for cloud-based enterprise technology, making it a global leader in database management systems, cloud computing, and enterprise software.

Controversies:

-**Leadership Style**: Ellison's autocratic leadership style, while effective, has been a source of debate and criticism within the business and tech communities. Critics argue that his approach can be overly controlling and confrontational.

-**Business Tactics**: Ellison has faced criticism for his aggressive business tactics. Some have accused him of being too confrontational in his business dealings, which has occasionally created rifts in both his personal and professional relationships.

-**Extravagant Lifestyle:** Ellison's lavish lifestyle and extravagant spending have also been points of contention, drawing attention and criticism from various quarters.

Larry Ellison's legacy in the tech industry is characterized by his relentless pursuit of innovation, strategic business acumen, and the ability to foresee and adapt to technological shifts. His contributions have not only shaped Oracle's history but have also had a lasting impact on the broader technology landscape.

Impact on his life and business

Larry Ellison's impact on his life and business is a narrative of extraordinary ambition, strategic acumen, and a relentless drive for innovation. As the co-founder and the driving force behind Oracle Corporation, Ellison's journey from a modest beginning to becoming a titan of the tech industry is a testament to his vision and determination.

Founding Oracle

In 1977, Ellison, along with Bob Miner and Ed Oates, founded Software Development Laboratories, which later became Oracle. Inspired by an IBM research paper on relational databases, they created the first commercial SQL for large relational databases. Their early success included a contract from the CIA, leading to the birth of the first commercial relational database, Oracle 2, in 1979.

IPO and Oracle 7

Oracle's IPO in 1986 was a significant milestone, but the company faced challenges, including a quarterly loss in

1990 and sales accounting controversies. The release of Oracle 7 in 1992 was a turning point, widely acclaimed and adopted by banks, governments, and major corporations, propelling the company to new heights.

Strategic Acquisitions

Ellison's vision extended beyond software development. Oracle's growth was fueled by strategic acquisitions, including Sun Microsystems, Hyperion Solutions, Retek, Siebel Systems, and PeopleSoft. Through these acquisitions, Oracle was able to penetrate various markets and provide an extensive array of solutions.

Oracle Cloud Infrastructure

By the year 2020, Ellison's strategic vision had prepared Oracle to meet the increasing needs for cloud-based business technology. Significantly, Zoom Video Communications selected Oracle's Cloud

Infrastructure to bolster their services amidst the COVID-19 pandemic, which served as further endorsement of Ellison's strategic choices.

Larry Ellison's impact on his life and business is characterized by his visionary leadership, which transformed Oracle from a startup into a global tech giant, with a significant impact on the tech industry. His strategic acquisitions and early recognition of the internet's potential played a pivotal role in Oracle's success.

5

Philanthropy

Larry Ellison's philanthropic efforts reflect his deep commitment to societal advancement, particularly in the fields of healthcare, education, and environmental conservation. Through the Larry Ellison Foundation, he has expressed his belief in the duty to use personal wealth to make a real difference in the world.Here are some key areas of Ellison's philanthropy:

-**Healthcare**: Ellison has made significant contributions to medical research, including establishing the Ellison Medical Foundation which supported over 600 scientific programs related to aging. He also donated $200 million to establish the

Lawrence J. Ellison Institute for Transformative Medicine of USC.

-**Education**: His philanthropy extends to education, with donations to prestigious universities like Stanford and Harvard. Ellison believes that a good life depends on a good education, and he has invested in educational initiatives to support this belief.

-**Food Production and Conservation:** Ellison's interests in food production and conservation have led to support for initiatives that tackle the world's food challenges and protect natural habitats and endangered species.

-**The Giving Pledge**: Ellison is a signatory of The Giving Pledge, committing to give the majority of his wealth to philanthropic causes. He has reportedly donated more than $800 million over time through his foundation.

Ellison's philanthropy is driven by a desire to create sustainable change and to measure success by the impact on lives saved or supported. His investments are aimed at making a sustained difference in the world, addressing some of the most critical needs of our communities and our planet.

Ellison's charitable endeavors

Larry Ellison's charitable endeavors are a significant part of his legacy, reflecting his commitment to using his wealth for societal benefit. His philanthropy spans various domains, including healthcare, education, and environmental conservation.

Healthcare

Ellison has made substantial contributions to medical research, particularly in aging and age-related diseases. He founded the Ellison Medical Foundation and donated $200 million to establish the Lawrence J. Ellison Institute for Transformative Medicine at USC, aiming to revolutionize cancer treatment.

Education

Believing that "a good life depends on a good education," Ellison has donated to educational institutions like Stanford and Harvard. He has also invested in initiatives to improve the quality of education and make it accessible to more people.

Environmental Conservation

As a passionate wildlife conservationist, Ellison has supported organizations like the Jane Goodall Institute for chimpanzee conservation in Africa and the Wildlife Conservation Network for protecting endangered species.

Disaster Relief

Ellison has been involved in disaster relief efforts, including donations to the American Red Cross for California wildfires and contributions to Hurricane Sandy relief efforts and the Nepal earthquake relief fund.

The Giving Pledge

In 2010, Ellison joined The Giving Pledge, committing to give away the majority of his wealth to philanthropic causes. He has pledged to give away 95% of his wealth, demonstrating his dedication to making a lasting positive impact on society.

Larry Ellison's philanthropic philosophy is centered around making sustainable change and measuring success by the impact on lives saved or supported. His investments aim to create a sustained difference in the world, addressing critical needs of communities and the planet.

Support for education and research

Larry Ellison's support for education and research is a significant aspect of his philanthropic portfolio. His contributions have focused on advancing medical research, particularly in the field of aging and age-related diseases, as well as supporting educational initiatives that aim to revolutionize cancer treatment and other areas of healthcare.

Medical Research

Ellison has been a steady supporter of biomedical research through the Lawrence Ellison Foundation, previously known as the Ellison Medical Foundation. The foundation has provided more than $300 million in funding for research on aging, including studies on stem cells, longevity genes, and age-related diseases and disabilities.

In 2016, Ellison made a landmark donation of $200 million to establish the Lawrence J. Ellison Institute for Transformative Medicine at the University of Southern California. This institute is dedicated to developing innovative therapies that target cancer at the molecular level, with the goal of revolutionizing cancer treatment.

Education

Ellison's philanthropy extends to education, where he has supported various educational charities, including

Reach to Teach, which focuses on education in India. His belief in the transformative power of education is evident in his substantial donations to institutions like Stanford and Harvard, as well as the establishment of the Ellison

Institute for Transformative Medicine, which has an educational component to its mission.

Environmental Conservation and Disaster Relief

Beyond healthcare and education, Ellison's charitable work includes environmental conservation efforts, such as his support for the Jane Goodall Institute and the Wildlife Conservation Networ. He has also contributed to disaster relief efforts, including donations to the American Red Cross for California wildfires and the Nepal earthquake relief fund.

The Giving Pledge

Ellison is a signatory of The Giving Pledge, committing to give away the majority of his wealth to philanthropic causes. He has pledged to give away 95% of his wealth, demonstrating his dedication to making a lasting positive impact on society.

Larry Ellison's support for education and research is driven by a desire to create sustainable change and to measure success by the impact on lives saved or supported. His investments aim to create a sustained difference in the world, addressing some of the most critical needs of our communities and our planet.

Impact on society

Larry Ellison's impact on society is significant and multifaceted, extending well beyond his role as the co-founder of Oracle Corporation. His philanthropic work has touched various sectors, including medical research, education, wildlife conservation, and disaster relief, making a difference in the lives of many.

Philanthropy in Medical Research

Ellison's contributions to medical research are notable, particularly in aging and age-related diseases. He founded the Ellison Medical Foundation and made substantial donations to entities such as the Harvard Medical School and the University of California, San Francisco.

Advancements in Education

Ellison has donated millions to educational causes, including a $200 million gift to the University of Southern California to establish the Lawrence J. Ellison Institute for Transformative Medicine, aiming to revolutionize cancer treatment.

Wildlife Conservation

As a passionate wildlife conservationist, Ellison has supported organizations like the Jane Goodall Institute for chimpanzee conservation in Africa and the Wildlife

Conservation Network for protecting endangered species.

Disaster Relief Efforts

Ellison has been actively involved in disaster relief, contributing to the American Red Cross for California wildfires and supporting relief efforts for Hurricane Sandy and the Nepal earthquake.

The Giving Pledge

By joining The Giving Pledge, Ellison has committed to giving away 95% of his wealth to philanthropic causes, setting an example for other billionaires to follow.

Overall, Larry Ellison's philanthropic endeavors have had a profound impact on society, demonstrating his commitment to using his wealth and influence to create positive change and address some of the world's most pressing challenges.

6

The Maverick CEO

Larry Ellison, known as the Maverick CEO, is renowned for his unconventional approach to business and leadership. From the very beginning, Ellison was willing to take big risks and make bold decisions, setting him apart from his more cautious contemporaries. His maverick style is characterized by a constant search for industry disruption and innovation.

As the CEO of Oracle, Ellison's aggressive growth strategies, including a series of high-profile acquisitions, expanded Oracle's product line and market share. He was recognized for his candid and direct manner of expression.competitive spirit, often challenging competitors directly.

Ellison's maverick leadership extended to his personal life, where he indulged in hobbies like yacht racing and aviation, and even purchased nearly an entire Hawaiian island. His lifestyle and business maneuvers reflect a person who is not bound by conventional wisdom but instead charts his own course, both in life and in business. This maverick attitude has been a key factor in his success and has left a lasting impact on the tech industry.

Ellison's leadership style

Larry Ellison's leadership style is best described as autocratic, characterized by centralized decision-making with little input from team members. Known for taking total control of situations and making necessary actions, Ellison's assertive decision-making style has been instrumental in Oracle's success.

Ellison's approach to running Oracle often involved direct involvement in decision-making and strategic direction, demonstrating a clear vision for the company while maintaining tight control over its operations. Despite criticisms of being overly controlling, his autocratic style has undeniably contributed to Oracle's resilience in the competitive tech landscape.

His leadership journey reflects ambition, innovation, and a relentless drive, deeply rooted in his early experiences and the foundation of Oracle. Ellison's hands-on and autocratic style in the early days were pivotal in steering Oracle through turbulent times and laying the groundwork for its future success.

Ellison's decisiveness enables him to take challenging decisions quickly and confidently, without any hesitation or doubt.This confident leadership and bold decision-making have been key factors in his and Oracle's enduring success.

Impact on Oracle's culture

Larry Ellison's impact on Oracle's culture has been profound and enduring. As the co-founder, his leadership style and business philosophy have deeply influenced the company's values, operations, and strategic direction. Here are some key aspects of how Ellison shaped Oracle's culture:

Autocratic Leadership

Ellison's autocratic leadership style is characterized by centralized decision-making with little input from team members. This approach has driven Oracle's success in the competitive tech industry, setting a benchmark for leadership in the sector.

Innovation and Excellence

Under Ellison's guidance, Oracle developed a reputation for being a tough but rewarding place to work. The culture he cultivated prioritized performance, results, and a relentless pursuit of innovation.

Competitive Spirit

Ellison's competitive nature permeated Oracle's culture, fostering an environment where aggressive growth strategies and direct challenges to competitors were the norms.

Strategic Vision

Ellison's strategic vision for Oracle included a commitment to healthcare, as seen in his recent remarks about Nashville being the center of healthcare's future, reflecting his vision for Oracle's role in transforming the industry through technology.

Adaptability

Ellison's leadership ensured that Oracle remained adaptable, embracing changes such as the shift to cloud computing and the integration of various acquired companies into Oracle's ecosystem.

Larry Ellison's legacy at Oracle is characterized by a culture that embraces bold decisions, values innovation, and maintains a competitive edge in the tech industry.

Leadership lessons

Larry Ellison's leadership journey offers a wealth of lessons that can be valuable for anyone looking to understand the dynamics of effective leadership. Here are some key lessons drawn from Ellison's approach:

Be Visionary

Ellison's ability to see the bigger picture and his daring to work towards it has been central to Oracle's success. He taught the world to look at the future while others were focused on the present.

Never Stop Growing

Ellison's career is a testament to the power of continuous learning and growth. His competitive nature and passion for winning drove him to constantly push boundaries and innovate[1].

Embrace Competition

Known for his competitive spirit, Ellison never shied away from acknowledging and taking on competitors. This mindset has been crucial in Oracle's journey to becoming a leading tech firm.

Generosity

Despite his bold statements and aggressive actions, Ellison's charitable donations often remain private. He believes charity is a personal matter, reflecting a quality of humility.

Autocratic Leadership

Ellison's autocratic leadership style, characterized by centralized decision-making, has been a defining feature of his tenure at Oracle. This style has steered the company through various industry challenges.

Hiring Philosophy

Ellison believed in hiring the best people and giving them the freedom to excel in their roles. This approach has helped Oracle attract and retain top talent.

Transparency and Outspokenness

Ellison was known for his transparency and willingness to speak his mind, even if it meant ruffling feathers. This openness has been a hallmark of his leadership style.

Resilience

Ellison's journey teaches that setbacks are opportunities for growth. Each challenge faced by Oracle under his leadership was a stepping stone to greater success.

These lessons from Larry Ellison's leadership reflect a blend of ambition, strategic acumen, and a relentless drive for excellence. They serve as guiding principles for current and future leaders in any industry.

7

Acquisitions and Expansion

Larry Ellison's strategy for the growth of Oracle has been significantly marked by acquisitions and expansion. Here are some key points that highlight his approach:

-**Data Center Expansion**: Recently, Oracle announced plans to significantly expand its data center footprint. Ellison stated that Oracle is in the process of expanding 66 of its existing cloud data centers and building 100 new cloud data centers.

-**Cerner Acquisition**: Oracle's acquisition of Cerner for $28.3 billion is one of the largest in its history, marking a significant move into the healthcare IT space.

-**Growth Through Acquisition**: Ellison's vision for growth through acquisition has allowed Oracle to leverage its strengths and resources to expand into new markets and industries.

- **Strategic Acquisitions:** Over the years, Oracle has made over 100 acquisitions, including major companies like PeopleSoft, Siebel Systems, and Sun Microsystems. This strategy has not only eliminated competitors but also introduced new technologies and talents integral to Oracle's innovation and expansion efforts.

Ellison's approach to acquisitions and expansion reflects his ability to adapt to industry trends and his foresight in positioning Oracle as a leader in the tech industry.

Oracle's growth strategy

Larry Ellison, the Chairman and CTO of Oracle, has been instrumental in shaping Oracle's growth strategy. Here are some key points about Oracle's recent strategic developments under Larry Ellison's leadership:

-**Generative AI Integration:** Oracle is embedding generative AI (GenAI) into its cloud services portfolio. This initiative aims to help customers and society tackle significant challenges by improving services like food production, healthcare, and application development.

-**Infrastructure Advancements:** Oracle's Gen2 Cloud Infrastructure (OCI) uses advanced networking technologies like ultrafast remote data memory access (RDMA) and connects NVIDIA GPUs in superclusters. This infrastructure is designed to train generative AI models efficiently, offering speed and cost advantages.

-**Application Development**: Oracle is shifting towards using GenAI tools for application development. For instance, Oracle APEX's application generator allows for faster development with smaller teams and reduces security flaws by generating code automatically based on developer prompts.

-**Strategic Acquisitions**: Since 2004, Ellison has led Oracle through a series of strategic acquisitions to increase market share, spending over $25 billion in three years to acquire companies that enhance Oracle's software capabilities.

-**Focus on Value Addition**: Oracle's strategy also involves adding more value to existing customers by expanding beyond ERP to industry-specific software, thus enhancing their offerings to mid-market and large companies.

These strategies reflect Oracle's commitment to innovation and efficiency, with Larry Ellison at the forefront of the company's visionary approach to growth and technology.

Integration of acquired companies

Larry Ellison's strategy for integrating acquired companies has been a cornerstone of Oracle's growth and success. Below are several principal elements of his strategy:

-**Visionary Approach:** Ellison's vision for growth through acquisition is based on his deep understanding of the technology landscape and his ability to identify potential synergies between companies.

He holds the conviction that Oracle can augment its product suite and deliver a more complete solution to its clientele by acquiring businesses that offer products or services that complement its own.

-**Expanding Product Portfolio**: Oracle has broadened its range of offerings by acquiring companies that specialize in different areas of technology. For instance, the acquisition of Sun Microsystems in 2010 allowed Oracle to become a one-stop-shop for hardware, software, and database solutions.

-**Market Entry and Dominance**: Instead of building products from scratch or competing head-on with established players, Ellison has often opted to acquire companies that already have a strong foothold in specific markets. This strategy has helped Oracle to quickly gain access to new markets and customers, diversify its revenue streams, and strengthen its position in the tech industry.

-**Vertical Integration:** Ellison's strategic business moves have also focused on vertical integration, where Oracle acquires companies that provide complementary products or services. This approach has enabled Oracle to offer integrated solutions across various industries.

Ellison's methodical and strategic approach to acquisition and integration has played a significant role in Oracle's expansion and dominance in the tech sector.

Challenges and opportunities

Larry Ellison, the co-founder of Oracle Corporation, has faced numerous challenges and seized various opportunities throughout his career. Here are some of the key challenges and opportunities that have marked his journey:

Challenges:

-**Market Competition:** Ellison has navigated Oracle through intense competition in the tech industry, particularly against rivals like SAP and Microsoft.

-**Technological Evolution:** Keeping pace with rapid technological changes and innovation has been a constant challenge.

-**Economic Fluctuations**: Global economic downturns, such as the dot-com bubble burst, have tested Oracle's resilience and Ellison's leadership.

-**Legal and Regulatory Issues**: Oracle has faced various legal battles and regulatory scrutiny, which have posed challenges for Ellison's strategic planning.

Opportunities:

-**Strategic Acquisitions:** Ellison has capitalized on the opportunity to grow Oracle through strategic acquisitions, expanding the company's product portfolio and market reach.

-**Cloud Computing:** The shift towards cloud computing has been a significant opportunity for Oracle to evolve and offer new services.

-**Global Expansion**: Ellison has led Oracle's expansion into emerging markets, providing growth opportunities beyond saturated Western markets.

-**Innovation and R&D**: Investing in research and development has allowed Oracle to stay at the forefront of technological advancements and maintain a competitive edge.

Ellison's approach to obstacles is straightforward: he faces them head-on, viewing challenges as opportunities to learn and grow. This persistence has been instrumental in achieving success beyond expectations. His leadership style, characterized by an autocratic approach, has shaped Oracle's strategic direction and culture, contributing to its position as a leading technology firm.

8

The Battle with Microsoft

It seems you're referring to the historical rivalry between Larry Ellison, the co-founder and CEO of Oracle Corporation, and Microsoft. This rivalry was particularly intense during the late 1990s and early 2000s, a period marked by fierce competition and legal battles in the tech industry.

Larry Ellison was known for his critical views of Microsoft and its then-chairman, Bill Gates. He openly accused Microsoft of engaging in unfair business practices and even funded investigations into groups that were supporting Microsoft during its antitrust battle with the U.S. government. Ellison's actions were part of a broader narrative of competition and conflict between Oracle and Microsoft, two giants in the software industry.

Ellison's rivalry with Bill Gates

The rivalry between Larry Ellison and Bill Gates is a well-documented chapter in the history of technology. It spans over four decades, with both titans founding their respective companies, Oracle and Microsoft, around the same time and with similar goals for the future.

Larry Ellison's Oracle went public on March 12, 1986, and Microsoft followed the next day. Microsoft's IPO was so successful that it doubled Oracle's market cap, setting the stage for a long-standing competition where Microsoft often came out on top.

Ellison has been vocal about his views on Microsoft and Bill Gates, often criticizing Gates for what he perceived as unfair business practices and a monopolistic approach to the software industry. He accused Gates of being a "villainous copier of technology with a misguided vision of the computer industry" and even referred to him as a "liar" regarding Microsoft's record of innovation.

The rivalry extended beyond business and into personal wealth, with Ellison driven by the ambition to surpass Gates in terms of net worth. A recent development suggests that Ellison may finally achieve this long-sought goal due to the financial implications of Bill Gates' divorce, potentially allowing Ellison to out-rank Gates by a significant margin.

Their feud was not just about market dominance but also about differing visions for the future of computing. Ellison has criticized Gates' view of a future computing model with data centralized on mega servers, which contrasts with the current model that Microsoft dominates but aligns with Oracle's core business of selling databases that reside on servers.

This rivalry, while intense, has also been marked by moments of civility, with both men sharing a passion for tennis and occasionally being pleasant to each other at tournaments. However, the competitive spirit and the desire to outdo each other have been a defining feature of their relationship.

Larry Ellison's Oracle Corporation has been a key player in the competitive software industry for over four decades. His strategic vision and aggressive business tactics have helped Oracle become one of the world's largest software companies, specializing in database technology and cloud computing.

Ellison's approach to competition is characterized by his willingness to take risks and his focus on delivering value to customers. He has been known to outmaneuver rivals by identifying and exploiting market opportunities, which has allowed Oracle to maintain a strong position in the industry.

The rivalry between Oracle and Microsoft, in particular, has been intense, with Ellison often criticizing Microsoft's practices and policies. This competition has extended to other competitors like

SAP, another enterprise software company.

Ellison's contributions to the software industry are numerous, and he has played a key role in the development of technologies that have revolutionized how businesses store and access their data. His development legacy includes his hands-on approach to product development and his involvement in every aspect of Oracle's business, from product design to sales and marketing.

Impact on the tech industry

Larry Ellison, through his leadership at Oracle, has significantly shaped the tech industry. His direct impact includes pioneering advancements in database technology, championing cloud computing, and influencing enterprise software development. Ellison's competitive nature and strategic business moves have not only propelled Oracle to the forefront of the tech world but also challenged other industry leaders to innovate and adapt. His legacy is evident in the robust infrastructure and comprehensive cloud services that Oracle provides today, which continue to support businesses around the globe. Ellison's vision and contributions have undeniably left an indelible mark on the technology landscape.

9

Ellison's Personal Life

Larry Ellison, known for his remarkable contributions to the tech industry, has also led a vibrant personal life. Born on August 17, 1944, in New York City, he was adopted by his aunt and uncle after a bout of pneumonia at nine months old. He grew up in Chicago's South Shore and later moved to California, where he entered the tech world.

Ellison has been married four times: to Adda Quinn, Nancy Wheeler Jenkins, Barbara Boothe—with whom he has two children, David and Megan—and Melanie Craft. His personal interests extend to yachting, aviation, and tennis, and he's known for his ownership of 98% of

Lāna'i, the sixth-largest island in the Hawaiian Islands.

His philanthropic efforts are notable as well, with significant contributions to medical research and education. Despite his immense wealth and public persona, Ellison maintains a level of privacy about his personal affairs, focusing public attention more on his professional achievements and visionary leadership in technology.

Marriages, children, and relationships

Larry Ellison has had a dynamic personal life with multiple marriages and children. Here's a brief overview:

- **Marriages:**

-**Adda Quinn**: Ellison's first wife, whom he married in 1967. Their marriage ended in 1974.

-**Nancy Wheeler Jenkins**: His second wife, married in 1977 and divorced in 1978.

-**Barbara Boothe**: Ellison married Boothe in 1983, and they had two children before their divorce in 1986.

-**Melanie Craft:** Became Ellison's fourth wife in 2003. They divorced in 2010.

- Children:

-**David Ellison**: Larry Ellison's son, who dropped out of the University of Southern California to pursue a career in Hollywood. He has been involved in big flicks like Mission: Impossible —Ghost Protocol and Star Trek Into the Darkness. David is also the founder of Skydance Media.

-Megan Ellison: Ellison's daughter, who is also a significant figure in Hollywood, known for her work behind the scenes in film production.

- **Relationships**:

-Ellison has been known to have a relationship with Nikita Kahn, but details about his current relationship status are not widely publicized.

Ellison's personal life, while intriguing, is often kept private, with the focus primarily on his professional achievements and contributions to the tech industry.

Hobbies and passions

Larry Ellison is known for his diverse hobbies and passions that reflect his dynamic personality and wealth. Here are some of his well-known interests:

-**Yachting**: Ellison's passion for sailing is legendary. He has won the America's Cup, one of the most prestigious sailing competitions, through his team Oracle Team USA. His love for the sport has led to technological advances in sailing that have benefited the entire sport.

-Aviation: Ellison is an accomplished pilot and owns several aircraft, including fighter jets.

- **Tennis**: He is an avid tennis fan and owns the Indian Wells Tennis Garden in California, which hosts the annual BNP Paribas Open tennis tournament.

-Japanese Culture: Ellison has a deep appreciation for Japanese culture and architecture. His Woodside, California home is modeled after a Japanese emperor's palace, and he owns a significant collection of Japanese and samurai art[5]. He also owns a historic garden property in Kyoto, Japan[5].

-**Real Estate**: Beyond his interest in Japanese properties, Ellison has a passion for high-end real estate and owns numerous properties around the world, including nearly the entire Hawaiian island of Lānaʻi.

-**Philanthropy**: Ellison is also known for his philanthropic efforts, particularly in medical research and education.

These hobbies and passions not only showcase Ellison's varied interests but also his commitment to excellence and innovation, traits that have also defined his professional career.

Influence on his career

Larry Ellison's influence on his career and the broader technology industry is substantial. His journey from a challenging early life to becoming a tech visionary is a testament to his determination and innovative spirit. Here are some key points that highlight his influence:

-**Early Beginnings**: Despite dropping out of college, Ellison's coding skills and vision led him to recognize the potential of relational databases early on. This foresight allowed him to co-found Oracle and develop the first commercial SQL for large relational databases.

-**Oracle's Growth**: Ellison guided Oracle through its initial public offering and subsequent challenges, including a quarterly loss and sales accounting controversies. The release of Oracle 7 marked a turning point, as it was widely adopted by banks, governments, and major corporations, solidifying Oracle's market position.

-**Strategic Acquisitions**: Under Ellison's leadership, Oracle made several strategic acquisitions, such as Sun Microsystems and PeopleSoft, allowing the company to diversify its offerings and strengthen its market presence.

-**Cloud Computing**: Ellison's vision for cloud-based enterprise technology positioned Oracle to meet the growing demand in this space. The choice of Oracle Cloud Infrastructure by Zoom during the COVID-19 pandemic is a notable example of this strategic foresight.

-**Competitive Edge**: Ellison's legendary ability to outmaneuver rivals has been a hallmark of his career. He developed relational database systems that could run on any computer, giving Oracle an edge over competitors like IBM in the 1980s.

-**Beyond Oracle**: Ellison's influence extends beyond his company. His early recognition of the internet's potential and his contributions to database management systems have set industry precedents and inspired other companies, making him a significant figure in the technology landscape.

Ellison's career is a reflection of his relentless pursuit of innovation and excellence, which has not only shaped Oracle's success but also had a lasting impact on the technology industry as a whole.

10

Innovation and Disruption

Larry Ellison's role as an innovator and disruptor in the tech industry is well-documented and widely recognized. His strategic thinking and relentless pursuit of progress have led to several key developments:

-**Oracle Database**: Ellison's creation of the Oracle database management system was a game-changer. It transformed the way companies managed their data, making it faster and more efficient, and set a new standard for the industry.

-**Entrepreneurial Vision**: Ellison's entrepreneurial journey with Oracle began with the goal of creating a superior database management system. His aggressive and competitive leadership style pushed his team to achieve excellence, leading to Oracle's rapid rise as a tech giant.

-**Innovation at Oracle**: Ellison fostered a culture of innovation at Oracle, always encouraging his team to think outside the box. This approach resulted in the creation of innovative products, such as Oracle's cloud computing platform.

-**Disruptive Moves**: Ellison has made several disruptive moves that have shaped the tech industry. He co-founded NetSuite, the first SaaS company, and funded Marc Benioff's launch of Salesforce. He also led Oracle into enterprise applications and acquired Sun Microsystems when others were exiting hardware.

-**Software and Hardware Integration:** Ellison pioneered the idea of integrating software and hardware to work together, enhancing the performance and capabilities of Oracle's products.

-**Cloud Revolution:** Contrary to some reports, Ellison never ridiculed cloud computing; instead, he criticized half-hearted efforts by others. He was an early investor in cloud technologies, including NetSuite and Salesforce, and later developed the Oracle Autonomous Database, a groundbreaking technology with no direct competitors at the time.

-**ERP Leadership:** In a significant development, Oracle under Ellison's guidance became the worldwide leader in cloud ERP, a category that had been dominated by SAP for over 40 years.

Ellison's impact on the tech industry extends beyond Oracle. His vision and innovations have not only driven his company's success but also influenced the direction of the entire sector. His legacy is one of relentless innovation and strategic disruption, which continues to inspire and shape the future of technology.

Contributions to relational databases

Larry Ellison's contributions to relational databases have been pivotal in shaping the modern technology landscape. His work has led to several key advancements:

-**Co-Founding Oracle**: In 1977, Ellison co-founded Oracle Corporation, which quickly became a leader in database technology, thanks to his vision and leadership.

-**First Commercial SQL**: Under Ellison's guidance, Oracle developed the first commercial SQL for managing large relational databases, a significant milestone in the industry.

-**Oracle Database**: The Oracle database management system was revolutionary, becoming the first to support SQL and setting new standards for data storage, management, and analysis.

-**Commercial Viability**: Ellison's company created the world's first commercially viable relational database, transforming how businesses accessed and used data.

-**CIA Contract**: Oracle's early success included winning a contract from the U.S. Central Intelligence Agency (CIA) to develop a relational database management system (RDBMS), which further established the company's reputation and capabilities.

Ellison's foresight and innovative approach to database technology have had a lasting impact, making him a key figure in the history of relational databases.

Driving technological advancements

Larry Ellison has been a driving force behind numerous technological advancements, particularly through his ventures into autonomous technology. His vision for harnessing the power of artificial intelligence and machine learning aims to revolutionize various industries, from transportation to supply chain management.

Here are some key areas where Ellison's influence is evident:

-**Autonomous Vehicles**: Ellison's Autonomous Technology Ventures (ATV) focuses on self-driving cars, which use sensors, cameras, and AI algorithms to navigate without human intervention. This technology has the potential to improve safety, reduce traffic congestion, and optimize fuel consumption.

-Supply Chain Automation: Ellison sees great potential in automating supply chains with AI-powered algorithms. This can streamline operations, improve efficiency, and reduce costs, leading to faster order fulfillment and enhanced customer satisfaction.

-**Autonomous Drones and Boats:** Beyond cars, Ellison's ventures also explore the use of autonomous technology in drones and boats, aiming to create more efficient and safer systems for transportation and logistics[1].

-**AI-driven Autonomy**: Ellison's focus on AI-driven autonomy is not limited to vehicles; it extends to robots and other automated systems that can perform tasks with minimal human intervention.

Ellison's commitment to innovation and his investments in autonomous technologies reflect his ongoing influence in driving the future of the tech industry.

Vision for the future of technology

Larry Ellison's vision for the future of technology is centered around the transformative potential of generative AI. At Oracle CloudWorld 2023, he discussed how generative AI can generate language, images, music, code, and even drugs, and how Oracle is leveraging this technology to enhance its cloud infrastructure, database, application development, and data intelligence platforms.

Ellison highlighted Oracle's RDMA network, autonomous database, Apex application generator, and vector database as key enablers for faster, cheaper, and more secure AI training and deployment. He also emphasized the societal impact of generative AI, tackling big world problems in healthcare, security, and agriculture.

His vision extends beyond enterprise applications to significant societal change, driven by Oracle's technology foundations, including wide-scale cloud infrastructure, autonomous databases, and large datasets. Ellison believes that generative AI is the most important new computer technology, potentially the most impactful ever, and sees a worldwide race to build better AI for a better future.

11

The Legacy of Larry Ellison

Larry Ellison's legacy in the tech industry is monumental, marked by his pioneering work in database technology and his leadership of Oracle Corporation. Here are some key elements that define his legacy:

-**Innovation**: Ellison co-founded Oracle and oversaw the development of the first commercially viable relational database, which became the largest supplier of database software globally.

-**Entrepreneurship**: His entrepreneurial spirit led Oracle to become a dominant force in the tech industry, providing a model for success in Silicon Valley.

-**Philanthropy**: Beyond business, Ellison's philanthropic endeavors have had a significant impact on society, particularly in medical research, wildlife conservation, education, and disaster relief.

-**Visionary Leadership**: Ellison's journey with Oracle showcases his ability to disrupt the technology industry and pave the way for new eras of innovation.

Ellison's contributions have not only shaped Oracle's success but also the entire landscape of technology, making him one of the most influential figures in the history of computing.

Impact on the tech industry and business world

Larry Ellison's impact on the tech industry and the business world is extensive and enduring. As the co-founder and long-time CEO of Oracle Corporation, he has been a pivotal figure in shaping the landscape of enterprise software and database management systems. Here are some key aspects of his influence:

-**Relational Database Revolution**: Ellison's Oracle was instrumental in popularizing relational databases, which have become the backbone of modern data management and storage. His work has enabled businesses to efficiently organize and retrieve large volumes of data, which is crucial for decision-making and operations.

-**Enterprise Software Leadership**: Under Ellison's direction, Oracle expanded its offerings to include not just databases but also a suite of enterprise software applications, making it a one-stop-shop for business computing needs.

-**Cloud Computing**: Ellison was an early proponent of cloud computing, recognizing its potential to transform the business world. Oracle's move into cloud services has allowed it to remain competitive in a rapidly changing technology environment.

-**Business Strategy**: Known for his aggressive business tactics, Ellison has led Oracle through a series of strategic acquisitions, expanding the company's reach and solidifying its position in the market.

-**Innovation and Disruption**: Ellison's commitment to innovation has kept Oracle at the forefront of technological advancements, continually disrupting the status quo and driving the industry forward.

-**Global Influence**: Ellison's vision and leadership have not only impacted Oracle but have also influenced the broader tech industry, inspiring a generation of entrepreneurs and business leaders.

Ellison's legacy is one of relentless pursuit of innovation, strategic business acumen, and a profound understanding of the transformative power of technology. His contributions continue to resonate throughout the tech industry and the business world at large.

Vision for the future

Larry Ellison's vision for the future of technology is deeply rooted in the potential of generative AI. At Oracle CloudWorld 2023, he emphasized how generative AI can create language, images, music, code, and even drugs, and how Oracle is integrating this technology into its cloud infrastructure, database, application development, and data intelligence platforms.

Ellison believes that generative AI is not just a breakthrough for the enterprise but also a catalyst for addressing big world problems in healthcare, security, and agriculture. He envisions Oracle's technology foundations—its extensive cloud infrastructure, autonomous databases, and vast datasets—as key drivers of societal change.

His perspective is that generative AI is the most important new computer technology, potentially the most impactful ever, and foresees a global race to develop better AI for a better future. Despite the risks associated with new technologies, Ellison is optimistic that, by and large, technology has improved human prosperity and comfort.

Enduring legacy

Larry Ellison's enduring legacy in the tech industry is a testament to his visionary leadership, innovative spirit, and significant contributions to database technology. As the co-founder of Oracle Corporation, Ellison has been a driving force behind the evolution of enterprise software and cloud computing. His journey from a university dropout to one of the world's wealthiest individuals is not only inspiring but also reflects his relentless pursuit of technological advancement and business excellence.

Ellison's assertive approach to management has played a pivotal role in navigating Oracle Corporation through the complexities of the tech industry, solidifying its status as a prominent player in the field.Despite criticisms, his approach has contributed to Oracle's success and resilience in the competitive tech landscape.

Moreover, Ellison's contribution to the field of Artificial Intelligence has been monumental, with his vision and passion advancing the development of AI technology for decades. His legacy in AI continues to influence the industry, reflecting his dedication to pushing the boundaries of what technology can achieve.

Overall, Larry Ellison's legacy is not just about the success of Oracle but also about the broader impact he has had on the tech world and the business community. His story is one of ambition, innovation, and the relentless pursuit of progress.

12

The Oracle Culture

Larry Ellison, the co-founder of Oracle Corporation, is known for his autocratic leadership style, which has been a significant factor in shaping the company's culture and success. His approach is characterized by centralized decision-making, with little input from team members, reflecting a clear vision for the company while maintaining tight control over its operations.

Ellison's leadership journey began with modest beginnings and a keen interest in computer technology. Despite dropping out of two universities, his passion for programming and software development led him to co-found Software

Development Laboratories in 1977, which was later renamed Oracle. His early life experiences and the foundation of Oracle offer a unique perspective on autocratic leadership.

Over the years, Ellison's leadership style has evolved, but it has remained hands-on and often autocratic, making critical decisions without extensive input from others. This style has steered Oracle through various industry challenges, ensuring its position as a leading technology firm.

Ellison's impact on Oracle's corporate identity and strategic direction is undeniable, and his leadership style continues to be a cornerstone of Oracle's operational ethos and a key driver of its success.

Unique culture and values

Larry Ellison's leadership style has had a profound impact on Oracle's organizational culture, shaping its values, behaviors, and operational ethos. His centralized leadership style, marked by direct oversight and decisive control, has been fundamental to defining Oracle's business philosophy and has significantly contributed to its achievements.

Ellison's unique culture and values can be summarized as follows:

-**Being Visionary:** Ellison saw the bigger picture and had the vision to work towards it, teaching the world to look at the future while others were focused on the present.

-**Never Stop Growing:** Ellison's philosophy is that growth isn't an option; it's a passion. He has always been driven by the courage to become the best and never stopped learning or growing.

-**Competitive Spirit**: Ellison is known for his competitive nature, always pushing boundaries and aiming for the championship, which has contributed significantly to Oracle's success.

-**Generosity**: Despite his bold statements and actions, Ellison keeps his charitable donations private, believing charity to be a personal matter.

-**Perseverance**: Ellison never mentions retirement, showing that he focuses on the present and organizational goals rather than the end.

These values have influenced various aspects of the company, from decision-making processes to employee engagement and morale. Ellison's style demonstrates that a strong, decisive leadership can guide a company through industry challenges and ensure its position as a leading technology firm.

Ellison's role in shaping it

Larry Ellison's role in shaping Oracle's culture has been pivotal. His autocratic leadership style has profoundly influenced the company's strategic direction, culture, and market position. Ellison's approach to running Oracle has often been marked by his direct involvement in decision-making and strategic direction, demonstrating a clear vision for the company while maintaining tight control over its operations.

Ellison's journey to becoming a renowned leader in the tech industry is a tale of ambition, innovation, and relentless drive. His leadership style, deeply rooted in his early experiences and the The establishment of Oracle provides a distinct perspective for examining autocratic leadership. Although Ellison's commanding leadership has faced scrutiny for being excessively authoritative, it has unmistakably played a role in Oracle's enduring success and adaptability within the fiercely competitive technology sector. His sharp emphasis on increasing sales and overtaking rivals has shaped the assertive nature of Oracle's corporate culture.As the founder and a major shareholder, Ellison's vision and priorities are likely to continue shaping Oracle's business strategies and corporate culture.

Ellison's contributions to the tech industry are numerous. He is recognized for creating the inaugural commercial relational database management system, a groundbreaking innovation that transformed the methods by which companies organize and handle data. He also played a key role in the development of cloud computing, which has become a critical component of modern business operations. His guidance has navigated Oracle through numerous challenges in the industry, maintaining its status as a foremost enterprise in the technology sector.

Impact on success

Larry Ellison's impact on Oracle's success is immense. His visionary leadership transformed Oracle from a startup into a global tech giant, significantly influencing the tech industry. Ellison's strategic acquisitions and early recognition of the internet's potential played a pivotal role in Oracle's growth.

Ellison's approach to business and technology has been characterized by a few key elements:

-**Innovation**: Ellison's foresight in the development of commercial relational database management systems revolutionized data storage and management.

-**Strategic Acquisitions:** Oracle's growth was fueled by strategic acquisitions, allowing the company to enter diverse markets and offer a wide range of solutions.

-**Adaptation to Market Changes**: Ellison's ability to adapt to market changes, such as the shift towards cloud computing, positioned Oracle to meet the growing demand for cloud-based enterprise technology.

-**Competitive Edge**: Ellison is known for his ability to outmaneuver rivals, which has been crucial in maintaining Oracle's competitive edge in the market.

Recent developments, such as Oracle's acquisition of Cerner, have faced challenges, but Ellison's commitment to overcoming these issues and transitioning to cloud-based systems demonstrates his ongoing influence on Oracle's strategic direction.Ellison's leadership style, marked by autocratic decision-making and a hands-on approach, has been a double-edged sword, attracting both admiration and criticism. Despite this, his impact on Oracle's success and resilience in the competitive tech landscape is undeniable. His contributions continue to shape Oracle's future, as seen in his recent comments about Nashville being the center of health care's future, reflecting his ongoing involvement in guiding Oracle's strategic ventures.

13

The Future of Oracle

Larry Ellison's vision for the future of Oracle is centered around leveraging cutting-edge technologies like generative AI to transform the company's cloud infrastructure, database, application development, and data intelligence platforms. In his keynote at Oracle CloudWorld 2023, Ellison highlighted the potential of generative AI to generate language, images, music, code, and even drugs, and how Oracle is incorporating this technology to enhance its offerings. Ellison's commitment to innovation is evident in Oracle's strategic direction, with a focus on developing a revolutionary new health management information system in the cloud. This system aims to be patient-centric, addressing the fragmentation of patient data across numerous databases, which can lead to inefficiencies and challenges in healthcare delivery.

Furthermore, Ellison has outlined plans for Oracle to play a significant role in transforming the healthcare industry by making healthcare records more unified and accessible at both the care provider and national levels. The acquisition of Cerner is a step towards this goal, combining Cerner's clinical capabilities with Oracle's enterprise cloud platform and analytics capabilities.

Ellison's future plans for Oracle also include a vision of building the future of global healthcare, indicating a shift towards a more service-oriented approach that could have a profound impact on how healthcare services are accessed worldwide.

Overall, Larry Ellison's influence on Oracle's future strategy appears to be focused on harnessing the power of AI and cloud computing to not only advance Oracle's technological capabilities but also to make a significant impact on industries like healthcare, potentially changing the way they operate on a global scale.

Ellison's successor and company direction

Larry Ellison, the co-founder of Oracle Corporation, stepped down from his role as CEO and was succeeded by Safra Catz and Mark Hurd as co-chief executives. Ellison remains an influential figure at Oracle as he took on the roles of chairman and chief technology officer.

As for the company's direction, Oracle continues to focus on its mission to help people see data in new ways, discover insights, and unlock endless possibilities[5]. The company is known for its comprehensive suite of enterprise software products and cloud services, including enterprise resource planning (ERP), human capital management (HCM), customer relationship management (CRM), and more. Oracle is committed to innovation, particularly in the cloud computing space, and maintains a strong emphasis on corporate responsibility and security practices.

Oracle's leadership under Catz and Hurd, along with Ellison's ongoing involvement, suggests a steady course for the company with a focus on growth in cloud computing and maintaining its position as a leading provider of enterprise software solutions.

Future prospects and challenges

Larry Ellison's future prospects seem to be closely tied to his vision for Oracle's role in a world increasingly driven by AI. At CloudWorld 2023, Ellison shared his expansive vision, which extends beyond enterprise solutions to tackle some of the world's significant challenges, including healthcare, security, and agriculture. His focus on generative AI suggests that he sees Oracle's technology foundations as drivers of societal change. Ellison's approach indicates a race to build better AI systems and a better future, acknowledging the associated risks but also the potential for technology to improve human prosperity and comfort.

As for the challenges, Oracle has faced some hurdles, particularly with its acquisition of Cerner. The company has encountered issues such as outages and systemic failures, which they are committed to addressing through cloud transition and system improvements. Additionally, Oracle's digital health records business, Cerner, has been losing market share in the US, highlighting the difficulties Oracle has faced since the acquisition.

Oracle's strategic direction includes a focus on cloud expansion and customer retention, despite global economic fluctuations and competitive pressures. The company's robust cloud and license revenue growth underscore its market dominance, and strategic acquisitions and R&D investments position Oracle for sustained innovation.

Larry Ellison's future prospects involve leveraging Oracle's capabilities to address large-scale problems with AI, while the challenges include integrating acquisitions like Cerner and maintaining market share in a competitive environment.

Plans for growth and innovation

Larry Ellison's plans for Oracle's growth and innovation are quite ambitious and multifaceted. Here are some key points:

-**Nashville Headquarters:** Ellison has announced plans to make Nashville the world headquarters for Oracle Corp. This move is strategic, placing Oracle at the heart of a major healthcare hub, which aligns with the company's ambitions in the industry.

-**Healthcare Focus:** The acquisition of Cerner for $28 billion in 2021 underscores Oracle's commitment to the healthcare sector. Ellison's vision includes leveraging Oracle's technology to revolutionize healthcare data management and patient care.

-**Global Expansion:** Oracle is expanding its cloud data center footprint globally, with plans to build out 100 new cloud data centers. This expansion will bolster Oracle's cloud infrastructure and services, ensuring they remain competitive and innovative.

-**Industry Innovation Lab:** Oracle's Industry Innovation Lab is a space where customers and partners can collaborate to ideate and innovate solutions to complex challenges across various industries. This initiative reflects Oracle's commitment to fostering innovation and co-creation.

-**Product and Service Innovation**: Oracle is focused on creating a product and service innovation engine. This involves strategic alignment, mature technical capabilities, and the right market timing to ensure that great ideas become successful products or services.

-**Continuous Innovation**: Oracle emphasizes the importance of continuous innovation across the product and service lifecycle. This approach is designed to drive success and maintain a competitive edge in the market.

Overall, Larry Ellison's plans for Oracle involve significant investments in healthcare, global infrastructure expansion, and fostering a culture of innovation that encourages collaboration and co-creation.

14

Ellison's Investments

Larry Ellison, known for his strategic and diverse investments, has a portfolio that includes a variety of asset classes. Here are some highlights of his investments:

-**Tesla**: In December 2018, Ellison invested $1 billion in Tesla, acquiring three million shares and a 1.7 percent stake in the company. This investment made him the second-largest individual shareholder behind Elon Musk.

-**Real Estate**: Ellison has a significant interest in real estate, owning properties in Silicon Valley, Lake Tahoe, and even most of the Hawaiian island of Lanai. His real estate portfolio includes a collection of homes, tennis courts, ranches, beaches, and gardens in Japan.

-**Sports**: He invested $60 million in Kosmos Tennis in October 2019, reflecting his interest in sports-related ventures.

-**Theranos**: Ellison was an early investor in the biotech company Theranos during a Series C funding round in 2006, although the company was later involved in a high-profile legal case.

-**Other Ventures**: Ellison's investments are not limited to the above; he also has stakes in other database companies, educational platforms, and luxury real estate, contributing to his substantial wealth.

Ellison's investment strategy is characterized by a mix of technology, luxury assets, and ventures that align with his personal interests and business acumen. His ability to identify and invest in promising companies and sectors has been a significant factor in his success as a businessman and investor.

Investments in various sectors

Larry Ellison's investments span across various sectors, reflecting his diverse interests and business acumen. Here are some of the sectors where he has made significant investments:

-**Technology**: Ellison's most notable investment is in **Tesla**, where he acquired a 1.7 percent stake by investing $1 billion in December 2018. He is the second-largest individual shareholder behind Elon Musk.

-**Real Estate:** He has a substantial real estate portfolio, including properties in

Silicon Valley, Lake Tahoe, and most of the Hawaiian island of Lanai. His holdings include luxury homes, tennis courts, ranches, beaches, and gardens in Japan.

-**Sports**: In October 2019, Ellison invested $60 million in Kosmos Tennis, indicating his interest in sports-related ventures.

-**Healthcare**: Ellison's investments in healthcare are evident from Oracle's acquisition of Cerner, a provider of digital health records, for $28 billion in 2021.

-**Other Ventures**: Ellison's investment portfolio also includes stakes in other database companies, educational platforms, and luxury real estate, contributing to his substantial wealth.

Ellison's strategic investments in these sectors not only diversify his wealth but also align with his vision for innovation and growth in key areas of the global economy.

Role as a venture capitalist

Larry Ellison's role as a venture capitalist extends beyond his executive duties at Oracle, showcasing his keen interest in supporting innovative startups and disruptive technologies. Here are some key points about his venture capitalist activities:

-**Strategic Investments**: Ellison has made strategic investments in various sectors, particularly in technology companies like Tesla, where he is a significant shareholder.

-**Support for Innovation**: He often invests in companies that align with his vision for the future, such as his investment in the healthcare sector through Oracle's acquisition of Cerner.

-**Risk-Taking**: Ellison is known for taking calculated risks, investing in companies like Theranos, which, despite its later issues, showed his willingness to support bold ideas.

-**Diverse Portfolio:** His portfolio is diverse, including real estate, sports, and technology, reflecting his broad interests and belief in cross-industry innovation.

-**Influence and Mentorship:** As a venture capitalist, Ellison not only provides financial backing but also offers guidance and mentorship to the companies he invests in, leveraging his extensive experience in building and scaling businesses.

Overall, Larry Ellison's role as a venture capitalist is characterized by his commitment to innovation, his strategic investment choices, and his influence in guiding the next generation of technology companies. He continues to be a prominent figure in the venture capital world, shaping the direction of new ventures with his insights and experience.

Impact on the tech industry

Larry Ellison, co-founder and former CEO of Oracle Corporation, is widely regarded as one of the most influential figures in the history of the tech industry. His visionary leadership, bold strategic decisions, and unwavering commitment to innovation have left an indelible mark on the industry landscape.

Oracle's Rise to Dominance

Under Ellison's guidance, Oracle transformed from a small startup into a global software giant. His relentless focus on product development and customer satisfaction propelled Oracle to become the leading provider of database management systems (DBMS). Oracle's database software became the backbone of countless enterprise applications, empowering businesses to manage and analyze vast amounts of data.

Cloud Computing Pioneer

Ellison recognized the transformative potential of cloud computing early on. He led Oracle's efforts to develop Oracle Cloud Infrastructure (OCI), a comprehensive cloud platform that provides businesses with a scalable, secure, and cost-effective environment to deploy and manage their applications and data. Today, OCI is a major player in the cloud computing market, competing with Amazon Web Services (AWS) and Microsoft Azure.

Open Source Advocacy

Ellison has been a vocal advocate for open source software. He believes that open source promotes innovation and collaboration within the tech industry. Oracle has made significant contributions to the open source community, including the development of popular open source projects such as MySQL, Java, and OpenOffice.

Philanthropy and Social Impact

Beyond his business endeavors, Ellison is also known for his philanthropy and social impact initiatives. He has contributed billions of dollars to a variety of initiatives, encompassing educational programs, medical research, and the conservation of the environment. Ellison's philanthropic efforts have made a tangible difference in the lives of countless people around the world.

Legacy and Impact

Larry Ellison's significant influence within the technology industry cannot be overstated. His visionary leadership, strategic acumen, and commitment to innovation have shaped the industry in profound ways. Oracle's database software and cloud platform have become essential tools for businesses of all sizes, and his advocacy for open source has fostered a more collaborative and innovative tech ecosystem. Ellison's legacy will continue to inspire generations of tech entrepreneurs and innovators for years to come.

Key Contributions to the Tech Industry:

·Led Oracle to become the dominant player in the database management systems market

· Pioneered the development of Oracle Cloud Infrastructure, a major cloud computing platform

- Promoted open source software and made significant contributions to the open source community
- Engaged in philanthropy and social impact initiatives, making a positive difference in the world

15

The Power of Data

Larry Ellison, co-founder and former CEO of Oracle Corporation, is a visionary leader who has long recognized the immense power of data. He believes that data is the lifeblood of modern businesses and that harnessing its potential can lead to transformative outcomes.

Data-Driven Decision Making

Ellison emphasizes the importance of data-driven decision making. He believes that businesses should leverage data to gain insights into their customers, operations, and markets. By analyzing data, businesses can make informed decisions that are more likely to lead to success.

Data Democratization

Ellison is also a strong advocate for data democratization, the idea that data should be accessible and usable by everyone in an organization, not just data scientists and analysts. He believes that empowering employees with data can lead to better decision making at all levels of the organization.

Oracle's Data Management Solutions

Oracle has developed a comprehensive suite of data management solutions to help businesses harness the power of data. These solutions include:

· **Oracle Database**: A powerful and scalable database management system that can handle vast amounts of data

· **Oracle Analytics**: A suite of tools for data analysis, visualization, and reporting

- **Oracle Machine Learning**: A platform for developing and deploying machine learning models
- **Oracle Autonomous Database:** A self-driving database that automates many administrative tasks, freeing up IT staff to focus on more strategic initiatives

Customer Success Stories

Numerous Oracle customers have achieved significant success by leveraging Oracle's data management solutions. For example:

- **Walmart**: Uses Oracle Database to manage its vast inventory and customer data, enabling it to provide personalized shopping experiences and improve supply chain efficiency.
- **AT&T**: Uses Oracle Analytics to analyze network data and identify potential outages, reducing downtime and improving customer satisfaction.

- **AstraZeneca**: Uses Oracle Machine Learning to develop predictive models for drug discovery, accelerating the development of new treatments.

Larry Ellison has been a driving force in the tech industry for decades. His vision for the power of data has shaped Oracle's product development and has helped countless businesses achieve success. Oracle's data management solutions empower organizations to harness the potential of data to make better decisions, improve operations, and gain a competitive advantage in the digital age.

Importance of data and its potential

Larry Ellison, co-founder and former CEO of Oracle Corporation, is a visionary leader who has long recognized the immense importance of data and its transformative potential. He believes that data is the lifeblood of modern businesses and that harnessing its power can lead to unprecedented opportunities.

Data-Driven Decision Making

Ellison emphasizes the importance of data-driven decision making. He believes that businesses should leverage data to gain insights into their customers, operations, and markets. By analyzing data, businesses can make informed decisions that are more likely to lead to success.

Data Democratization

Ellison is also a strong advocate for data democratization, the idea that data should be accessible and usable by everyone in an organization, not just data scientists and analysts. He believes that empowering employees with data can lead to better decision making at all levels of the organization.

The Potential of Data

Ellison believes that data has the potential to transform businesses in a number of ways, including:

•**Improving customer experiences:** Businesses can use data to better understand their customers' needs and preferences, enabling them to provide more personalized and relevant products and services.

• **Optimizing operations:** Data can be used to identify inefficiencies and bottlenecks in business processes, allowing businesses to streamline their operations and improve productivity.

• **Developing new products and services:** Data can be used to identify new market opportunities and develop innovative products and services that meet the evolving needs of customers.

· **Gaining a competitive advantage:** Businesses that effectively leverage data can gain a competitive advantage over those that do not, by making better decisions, improving their operations, and developing new products and services. Larry Ellison is a visionary leader who has been a driving force in the tech industry for decades. His vision for the importance of data and its potential has shaped Oracle's product development and has helped countless businesses achieve success. Oracle's data management solutions empower organizations to harness the potential of data to make better decisions, improve operations, and gain a competitive advantage in the digital age.

Predictions for the future

Larry Ellison, co-founder and former CEO of Oracle Corporation, is known for his bold predictions about the future of technology.Highlighted below are several of his most distinguished forecasts:

· **The rise of autonomous systems**: Ellison believes that autonomous systems, which can operate independently without human intervention, will become increasingly prevalent in the future. He predicts that autonomous systems will be used to automate a wide range of tasks, from driving cars to managing businesses.

· **The decline of traditional software:** Ellison predicts that traditional software, which requires manual installation and maintenance, will eventually be replaced by cloud-based software that is accessed on demand over the internet. He believes that cloud-based software is more scalable, secure, and cost-effective than traditional software.

· **The importance of data**: Ellison believes that data will become increasingly important in the future. He predicts that businesses that effectively leverage data to gain insights into their customers, operations, and markets will be more successful than those that do not.

· **The convergence of technologies**: Ellison predicts that different technologies, such as artificial intelligence, machine learning, and blockchain, will increasingly converge in the future. He believes that this convergence will lead to the development of new and innovative products and services.

· **The impact of technology on society**: Ellison believes that technology will have a profound impact on society in the future. He predicts that technology will lead to both positive and negative changes, and that it is important to be prepared for both.

Larry Ellison is a visionary leader who has been a driving force in the tech industry for decades. His predictions for the future provide valuable insights into the potential and challenges that lie ahead. By understanding and preparing for these changes, businesses and individuals can position themselves for success in the digital age.

Implications for businesses and society

Larry Ellison's predictions for the future have significant implications for businesses and society as a whole. Here are some of the most notable implications:

Businesses

· **Need to adapt to autonomous systems:** Businesses will need to adapt to the rise of autonomous systems by developing new strategies for managing and using these systems. This may involve retraining employees, developing new business models, and investing in new technologies.

•**Move to cloud-based software:** Businesses will need to move to cloud-based software in order to remain competitive. Cloud-based software is more scalable, secure, and cost-effective than traditional software, and it allows businesses to access their applications and data from anywhere.

· **Focus on data**: Businesses will need to focus on effectively leveraging data to gain insights into their customers, operations, and markets. This may involve investing in data management solutions, hiring data scientists, and developing data-driven strategies.

·**Prepare for the convergence of technologies**: Businesses will need to prepare for the convergence of different technologies, such as artificial intelligence, machine learning, and blockchain. This may involve investing in research and development, partnering with other companies, and developing new products and services.

Society

· **Impact on employment**: The rise of autonomous systems may have a significant impact on employment. Some jobs may be automated, while new jobs may be created to develop, maintain, and manage autonomous systems.

· **Need for new skills:** The convergence of different technologies will create a need for new skills in the workforce. Individuals will need to develop skills in areas such as data science, artificial intelligence, and machine learning.

·**Ethical considerations:** The development and use of new technologies raise ethical considerations. For example, it is important to consider the ethical implications of using autonomous systems in areas such as healthcare and criminal justice.

16

The Wisdom of Larry Ellison

Larry Ellison, co-founder and former CEO of Oracle Corporation, is one of the most successful and influential figures in the tech industry. Over the years, he has shared many valuable insights and lessons learned through his experiences. Here are some of the most notable nuggets of wisdom from Larry Ellison:

•Embrace the possibility of failure. Ellison sees failure as a critical component of growth. He inspires people to welcome challenges and view mistakes as opportunities for learning.

-Diligence and persistence are key. Ellison is renowned for his relentless dedication to his work. He is of the opinion that diligence and steadfastness are crucial to achieving success.

-Prioritize the consumer.Ellison holds the view that companies should prioritize satisfying their customers' requirements. He asserts, "Your customers will support you if you support them."

-Evolve or become obsolete. Ellison is convinced that for companies to remain in the race, innovation is indispensable. He advocates for continuous innovation and the creation of novel products and services.

Trust in your own abilities.Ellison champions the importance of self-belief. His guidance is, "Belief in oneself is a prerequisite for others to place their trust in you."

-Disregard the skeptics. Ellison has frequently been challenged by skeptics and naysayers. He maintains that one should stay focused on their path despite criticism.

-Contribute to society. Ellison, known for his philanthropy, has contributed significantly to various initiatives. He emphasizes the importance of contributing to society and effecting positive change.

Larry Ellison's insights offer a wealth of knowledge for those seeking to excel in business and life. Heeding his counsel can enhance your prospects for success and enable you to contribute positively to the world.

Insights on leadership and success

Larry Ellison, co-founder and former CEO of Oracle Corporation, is one of the most successful and influential leaders in the tech industry. Over the years, he has shared many valuable insights on leadership and success.Consider these significant points:

·Vision is imperative for leadership. Ellison asserts that for leadership to be effective, a distinct and persuasive vision is indispensable. He contends, "Leadership is unattainable without a vision."

· "A leader must be able to communicate effectively." Ellison believes that leaders must be able to communicate their vision and goals to their team in a clear and -

·Clarity in communication is crucial. He

emphasizes, "Leadership is ineffective without the ability to communicate."

·Decisiveness is essential for leadership. Ellison holds that the capacity to make difficult choices is a hallmark of leadership, even if those choices aren't widely accepted. He advises, "Without the ability to decide on tough matters, one cannot lead."

·Delegation is key to leadership.Ellison advocates for leaders to assign responsibilities to their team and enable them to make decisions. He suggests, "Business growth is hindered without the ability to delegate."

·The power to motivate is fundamental to leadership. Ellison believes that the ability to drive and uplift team members is a core attribute of a leader.He asserts, "A leadership position is unattainable without the drive to inspire and motivate."

•Learning from errors is vital for leadership. Ellison considers the ability to learn from one's mistakes as a cornerstone for leadership development. He states, "Leadership is unfeasible if one does not take lessons from their mistakes."

• "A leader must be able to give back to the community." Ellison believes that leaders should use their success to make a positive impact on the world. He says, "If you can't give back to the community, you can't be a leader."

Larry Ellison's insights on leadership and success are a valuable resource for anyone who wants to achieve success in their career and life. By following his advice, you can increase your chances of becoming a successful leader and making a positive difference in the world.

Guiding principles and philosophies

Larry Ellison, co-founder and former CEO of Oracle Corporation, is a visionary leader who has shaped the tech industry for decades. His success is due in part to his adherence to a set of guiding principles and philosophies.These are a few of the key highlights:

•**Client-centric approach**: Ellison's perspective is that companies should prioritize the satisfaction of their clients. His philosophy is, "By looking after your clients, they, in turn, will look after you."

-**Continuous innovation:** Ellison advocates for the necessity of innovation as a means for companies to maintain their edge. He promotes the idea of ceaseless innovation and the creation of fresh offerings.

-**Unwavering diligence:** Ellison's reputation for his indefatigable commitment to work is well-known. He considers consistent effort and determination as fundamental to triumph.

•**Embracing risk:** Ellison is an advocate for risk-taking. He views it as a crucial element for attaining remarkable achievements.

-**The value of failure:** Ellison regards failure as a pivotal aspect of educational growth. He inspires individuals to venture into the unknown and not shy away from errors.

-**The importance of integrity:** Ellison holds integrity in high regard, deeming it indispensable for prosperity in both business and personal realms. His conviction is that without the presence of integrity, one essentially has nothing.

-**Philanthropic responsibility:** Ellison, a philanthropist, has made substantial donations to a multitude of causes. He believes in the significance of contributing to the community and fostering positive change globally.

Larry Ellison's guiding principles and philosophies have served him well throughout his career. Emulating his approach can enhance your prospects of achieving success in both your professional and personal endeavors.

Lessons from his experiences

Larry Ellison, co-founder and former CEO of Oracle Corporation, has had a long and successful career in the tech industry. Along the way, he has learned many valuable lessons that can benefit anyone who wants to achieve success in business and life. Here are some of the most notable lessons from Larry Ellison's experiences:

•**Venture boldly:** Ellison embraces the concept of risk-taking. He holds the conviction that embracing risks is crucial for monumental achievements. As an illustration, Ellison's choice to leave college and establish Oracle was a gamble that paid off significantly in his favor.

• **Work hard:** Ellison is known for his tireless work ethic. He believes that hard work and perseverance are essential for success. Ellison often works long hours and is always looking for ways to improve his products and services.

•**Innovate**: Ellison believes that innovation is essential for businesses to stay competitive. He encourages businesses to constantly innovate and develop new products and services. Oracle has a long history of innovation, and Ellison has been instrumental in the development of many of the company's most successful products.

· **Focus on the customer**: Ellison believes that businesses should always focus on meeting the needs of their customers. He says, "If you take care of your customers, they will take care of you." Oracle has a strong customer focus, and the company is known for its high-quality products and services.

· **Learn from your mistakes:** Ellison believes that failure is an essential part of the learning process. He advocates for individuals to embrace risk-taking and to not fear committing errors. Ellison has made many mistakes throughout his career, but he has learned from each one and used them to improve his business.

· **Give back to the community:** Ellison is a generous philanthropist who has donated billions of dollars to various causes. He believes that it is important to give back to the community and make a positive difference in the world. Ellison has supported many educational and environmental causes, and he has also donated money to disaster relief efforts.

Larry Ellison's experiences have taught him many valuable lessons about success in business and life. By following his example, you can increase your chances of achieving your own goals and making a positive impact on the world.

17

The Final Chapter

Larry Ellison, co-founder and former CEO of Oracle Corporation, is one of the most successful and influential figures in the tech industry. Over the course of his career, he has built a multi-billion dollar software empire and revolutionized the way businesses use and manage data.

Ellison's legacy extends far beyond his financial success. He is also known for his visionary leadership, his commitment to innovation, and his generous philanthropy. He has been a driving force behind the development of some of the most important technologies of our time, including the relational database management system and cloud computing.

Ellison's impact on the tech industry is undeniable. He has helped to shape the way we live and work in the digital age. His enduring legacy will serve as an inspiration for future generations of entrepreneurs and creative minds for many years ahead.

Key Contributions to the Tech Industry:

· Founded Oracle Corporation, one of the largest software companies in the world

·Developed the relational database management system, a fundamental technology for storing and managing data

· Pioneered cloud computing, a model for delivering software and services over the internet

·Invested heavily in research and development, leading to the creation of new technologies and products

·Mentored and inspired countless entrepreneurs and innovators

Philanthropy and Social Impact:

·Contributed a substantial sum, amounting to billions, towards diverse initiatives encompassing educational programs, health research, and the safeguarding of the environment.

· Founded the Ellison Medical Foundation, which supports biomedical research

· Established the Lawrence J. Ellison Institute for Transformative Medicine, which focuses on personalized medicine

· Played a significant role in supporting disaster relief activities globally.

Leadership and Vision:

· Known for his visionary leadership and ability to think big

· Encouraged a culture of innovation and risk-taking at Oracle

- Inspired employees to achieve their full potential
- Remained actively involved in Oracle's business long after stepping down as CEO

Larry Ellison's legacy is one of innovation, leadership, and philanthropy. He has made a profound impact on the tech industry and the world at large. His contributions will continue to shape the future of technology and inspire generations to come.

Lasting impact on the tech world

Larry Ellison, the co-founder and former CEO of Oracle Corporation, has left an indelible mark on the technology industry. Here are some key aspects of his lasting impact:

1.Database Management Systems (DBMS):

· Ellison is widely regarded as one of the pioneers of modern DBMS. Oracle's relational database management system (RDBMS), Oracle Database, has become a de facto standard in the enterprise computing landscape.

· His focus on data integrity, performance, and scalability revolutionized data management and set the foundation for countless applications.

2. Software-as-a-Service (SaaS):

· Oracle was among the early adopters of SaaS, a cloud-based software delivery model. Ellison recognized the potential of delivering software over the internet and invested heavily in its development.

· Oracle's SaaS offerings, such as Oracle Cloud ERP and CRM, have become popular choices for businesses seeking cost-effective and efficient enterprise solutions.

3. Cloud Computing:

· Ellison was an early proponent of cloud computing and saw its transformative potential. He guided Oracle's transition from an on-premises software provider to a cloud-based platform company.

· Oracle Cloud offers a comprehensive suite of services, including infrastructure-as-a-service (IaaS), platform-as-a-service (PaaS), and software-as-a-service (SaaS).

4. Innovation and Disruption:

· Ellison is known for his aggressive approach to innovation and his willingness to disrupt the status quo. He invested heavily in research and development to create new and innovative technologies.

· Oracle's technologies have pushed the boundaries of what is possible in enterprise software and have empowered businesses to achieve new levels of efficiency and productivity.

5. Leadership and Vision:

· Ellison's leadership was instrumental in shaping Oracle's culture and its unwavering focus on customer satisfaction. He instilled a sense of urgency and a desire to create products that solve real-world problems.

·His strong vision and determination have guided Oracle through multiple technological shifts and positioned it as a leader in the tech industry.

6. Philanthropy and Social Impact:

· Beyond his technological contributions, Ellison has made significant philanthropic contributions through the Ellison Medical Foundation and other organizations.

· His investments in medical research and environmental conservation reflect his commitment to making a positive impact on society.

Larry Ellison's lasting impact on the tech world is undeniable. His pioneering work in DBMS, his early adoption of SaaS and cloud computing, and his relentless pursuit of innovation have transformed the way businesses manage and leverage data. His leadership and vision have shaped the trajectory of Oracle and the broader technology industry, leaving a legacy that will continue to influence the future of technology.

Contributions to society

Larry Ellison, the co-founder of Oracle Corporation, has made significant contributions to society through his philanthropic endeavors. Here are some key areas where his generosity has had an impact:

1.**Medical Research**: Ellison has been a strong supporter of medical research, particularly in aging and age-related diseases. He founded the Ellison Medical Foundation and has donated millions to research institutions like Harvard Medical School and the University of California, San Francisco.

2.**Wildlife Conservation**: A passionate wildlife conservationist, Ellison donated $4 million to the Jane Goodall Institute to support chimpanzee conservation in Africa and has supported the Wildlife Conservation Network to protect endangered species.

3.In the realm of education, his impact has been substantial, exemplified by his generous endowment of $200 million to the University of Southern California, which facilitated the creation of the Lawrence J.

4.**Disaster Relief**: Ellison has been involved in disaster relief efforts, donating to the American Red Cross for California wildfires relief, Hurricane Sandy relief efforts, and the Nepal earthquake relief fund.

5.**The Giving Pledge:** In 2010, Ellison joined the Giving Pledge, committing to give away 95% of his wealth to philanthropic causes, setting an example for other billionaires.

Overall, Larry Ellison's philanthropy has had a profound impact on various sectors, including health, education, environment, and disaster relief, improving countless lives and inspiring others to give back to society.

Enduring legacy and place in history

Larry Ellison's enduring legacy and his place in history are marked by his pioneering contributions to the technology industry and his transformative impact on modern business practices. Here are some key aspects of his legacy:

1.**Co-founder of Oracle Corporation:** Ellison co-founded Oracle in 1977, which became a leading provider of database software and technology, cloud-engineered systems, and enterprise software products.

2.**Revolutionizing Database Management:** Ellison's work has revolutionized the way data is stored, managed, and analyzed, impacting fields such as finance, healthcare, and retail.

3.**Inspirational Entrepreneur**: His journey from a university dropout to one of the world's wealthiest individuals serves as an inspiration to aspiring entrepreneurs and tech enthusiasts.

4.**Tech Visionary:** Ellison's vision and leadership have been instrumental in shaping the evolution of Oracle, demonstrating the transformative potential of innovation in the digital age.

5.**Philanthropy**: Beyond technology, Ellison's philanthropic efforts in medical research, education, and wildlife conservation have made a significant social impact.

Overall, Larry Ellison's legacy is not only defined by his success with Oracle but also by his broader contributions to society and his role as a visionary in the tech world.

Conclusion

In the final analysis, Larry Ellison's biography is a testament to the power of vision, innovation, and relentless pursuit of excellence. From the early days of Oracle, navigating the nascent world of database management, to becoming a titan of technology and a beacon of philanthropy, Ellison's journey embodies the quintessential American dream. His legacy is etched not only in the silicon of processors but also in the hearts of those he has inspired and the lives he has transformed. As we close the pages of this book, we reflect on a man whose life story is a mosaic of ambition, intellect, and generosity—a legacy that will continue to influence generations to come. Ellison's story is far from over, but the chapters recounted here serve as a powerful reminder that the paths we carve can lead to destinations beyond our wildest imaginations. **Larry Ellison** stands as a paragon of the transformative potential that individuals have in shaping our world, ensuring his place in the annals of history not merely as a figure of the past but as a continuing source of inspiration for the future.

www.ingramcontent.com/pod-product-compliance
Lightning Source LLC
Chambersburg PA
CBHW071919210526
45479CB00002B/479